W9-AZW-808

EXPLORING DINOSAURS & PREHISTORIC CREATURES

PSITTACOSAURUS

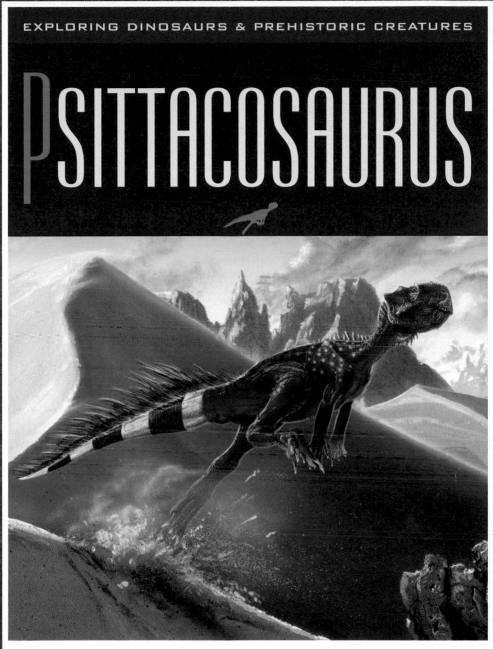

By Susan H. Gray

THE CHILD'S WORLD®
CHANHASSEN, MINNESOTA

The Child's World

Published in the United States of America by The Child's World®
PO Box 326, Chanhassen, MN 55317-0326
800-599-READ
www.childsworld.com

Content Adviser:
Peter Makovicky,
PhD, Curator,
Field Museum,
Chicago, Illinois

Photo Credits: American Museum of Natural History Library: 12 (neg 410960), 18 (#7769); Bettmann/Corbis: 13; Kevin R. Morris/Corbis: 21; Jonathan Blair/Corbis: 22; Scott Olson/Getty Images: 15; The Natural History Museum, London: 4, 6, 7, 8, 9, 16; Michael P. Gadomski/Photo Researchers, Inc.: 20; Francois Gohier/Photo Researchers, Inc.: 23; Chris Butler/Science Photo Library/Photo Researchers, Inc.: 25; Roger Harris/ Science Photo Library/Photo Researchers, Inc.: 26; Albert Copley/Visuals Unlimited: 19.

The Child's World®: Mary Berendes, Publishing Director

Editorial Directions, Inc.: E. Russell Primm, Editorial Director; Katie Marsico, Associate Editor; Ruth Martin, Line Editor; Judith Shiffer, Assistant Editor; Matt Messbarger, Editorial Assistant; Susan Hindman, Copy Editor; Melissa McDaniel, Proofreader; Olivia Nellums, Fact Checkers; Tim Griffin/IndexServ, Indexer; Dawn Friedman, Photo Researcher; Linda S. Koutris, Photo Selector

Original cover art by Todd Marshall

The Design Lab: Kathleen Petelinsek, Design and Page Production

Library of Congress Cataloging-in-Publication Data
Gray, Susan Heinrichs.
  Psittacosaurus / by Susan H. Gray.
    v. cm. — (Exploring dinosaurs)
  Contents: Cleaning up—What is a Psittacosaurus?—The discovery of Psittacosaurus—Built to eat plants—Psittacosaurus and its relatives—The world of Psittacosaurus.
  ISBN 1-59296-237-8 (lib. bdg. : alk. paper) 1. Psittacosaurus—Juvenile literature. [1. Psittacosaurus. 2. Dinosaurs.] I. Title.
  QE862.O65G7457 2005
  567.915—dc22   2003027054

TABLE OF CONTENTS

CHAPTER ONE

4 Cleaning Up

CHAPTER TWO

7 What Is a *Psittacosaurus*?

CHAPTER THREE

11 The Discovery of *Psittacosaurus*

CHAPTER FOUR

16 Built to Eat Plants

CHAPTER FIVE

22 *Psittacosaurus* and Its Relatives

CHAPTER SIX

25 The World of *Psittacosaurus*

28 Glossary

28 Did You Know?

29 How to Learn More

30 The Geologic Time Scale

32 Index

CLEANING UP

P*sittacosaurus* (SIT-uh-koe-SAWR-uhss) awoke from her nap.

She blinked a couple of times and lifted her head. Her neck

was stiff from sleeping in an awkward position. She slowly got up

Compared to other plant-eating dinosaurs such as Stegosaurus *(STEG-oh-SAWR-uhss) and* Triceratops *(try-SEHR-uh-tops),* Psittacosaurus *was quite small. When the little prehistoric* **reptile** *stood on its hind legs, it still didn't measure as tall as most adult human beings!*

and then turned her head from the left to the right, stretching the muscles. She leaned forward, tensed her back, and stiffened her tail straight out behind her. Now that she had stretched, she was fully awake.

However, she didn't look so great. One side of her face was matted with damp leaves and pine needles, and a twig was stuck between two teeth. *Psittacosaurus* rose up on her back legs and began grooming. She bent her head down and swept her hand across her face. Most of the leaves and needles fell to the ground. She wiped her face again and again. Once her face was clean, *Psittacosaurus* began working on the twig.

She picked at it with her fingers, but it did not move. She shook her head violently, but the twig remained lodged in place. Then *Psittacosaurus* worked her lower jaw around, trying to loosen the

Psittacosaurus's birdlike beak was perfect for grasping and tearing tough prehistoric plant matter.

twig. She was getting nowhere when suddenly—ulp! The twig came

loose and slipped down the dinosaur's throat.

Psittacosaurus stood perfectly still for a second and then ran her

hand over her face one more time. Now she was all cleaned up and

ready to go exploring.

CHAPTER TWO

WHAT IS A *PSITTACOSAURUS*?

Psittacosaurus was a dinosaur that lived from about 120 million to 98 million years ago. Its name is taken from Greek words that mean "parrot lizard." The name refers to the dinosaur's parrotlike head.

This Psittacosaurus *skull is housed at the Natural History Museum in London, England. Although the shape of the dinosaur's head makes people think of a parrot, it's important to remember that* Psittacosaurus *was a reptile—not a bird.*

When people think about dinosaurs, they probably imagine huge prehistoric beasts that make elephants seem small in comparison. But not all dinosaurs were giants. Scientists once discovered a baby Psittacosaurus *skeleton that measured less than 1 foot (30 centimeters) long.*

Psittacosaurus was not a big dinosaur. From its snout to the tip

of its tail, an adult measured about 6.5 feet (2 meters) long. The

dinosaur's thick tail made up about half of that length. When the reptile reared up on its back legs, it stood 3.5 feet (1.1 m) tall. Scientists think that an adult *Psittacosaurus* might have weighed between 50 and 100 pounds (22.7 and 45 kilograms).

The reptile's back legs were longer than its front ones, but not by much. *Psittacosaurus* probably walked on two feet most of the time, but it could bend over and walk on all fours if necessary. Its hands each had four fingers. The innermost finger pointed slightly away from the other three. This might have made it possible for *Psittacosaurus* to grasp and hold things.

The most unusual feature of the dinosaur was its boxy, parrot-shaped head. At the back of the head was a bony ridge. Under the skin, powerful jaw muscles were attached to this ridge.

The front of the head was narrow and ended in a large, hard beak. The upper part of the beak was pointed and curved downward, overlapping the lower part. The dinosaur's teeth were set in the sides and back of the mouth, away from the beak. Its nostrils were high up on the head, and its eyes were large. Short horns stuck out from the dinosaur's cheeks.

Although later dinosaurs such as Triceratops *had horns above its beak and eyes,* Psittacosaurus *had horns that stuck out from its cheeks.*

CHAPTER THREE

THE DISCOVERY OF *PSITTACOSAURUS*

In the early 1900s, scientists all over the world were looking for dinosaur **fossils.** Some thought that Mongolia might be a good place to find them. Mongolia is a country that lies between Russia and China. Part of the country is made up of desert. Scientists thought that this part of the world might have been home to some early forms of life. They thought that hot, dry deserts might have been likely to **preserve** those early life-forms. One of these scientists was Henry Fairfield Osborn. He ran a museum in New York City.

In 1922, Osborn sent a team of scientists to Mongolia to search for fossils. Planning the trip was a nightmare. Sending a group of scientists to the other side of the world was not easy. They would need

Fossil hunting teams in Mongolia during the early 1900s faced several challenges. Apart from the climate and snakes, workers often had to rely upon camel trains to move supplies across the hot Mongolian desert.

lots of supplies and equipment. They would need to be able to protect themselves from bandits and poisonous snakes. And when they arrived, they would have to hire many Mongolian helpers. The scientists would need cooks, drivers, and people to dig, carry, and pack things.

Even with all their planning, the trip went badly. The afternoons brought terrible heat. Nights were so cold that the workers shivered in their beds. Men found snakes coiled under their blankets. Violent winds knocked over their tents. Pots and pans blew away. Bandits raided the camp. Natives accused the scientists of being spies and thieves.

Despite all of their problems, the men made some incredible

finds. They discovered several new dinosaurs and even found some dinosaur eggs. One of the team's helpers, a Mongolian driver named Wong, found a most unusual skeleton. It was from a dinosaur that had a boxy, parrotlike head.

In addition to naming Psittacosaurus, *Henry Osborn also named dinosaurs such as* Tyrannosaurus rex *(tie-RAN-uh-SAWR-uhss REX)*, Oviraptor *(OH-vih-RAP-tur)*, *and* Velociraptor *(vuh-LAHS-ih-RAP-tur)*.

The team sent the dinosaur's bones back to Osborn in New York. In 1923, Osborn wrote a paper about the animal, and he named it *Psittacosaurus*. Since that time, many *Psittacosaurus* remains have been found in Mongolia, China, and Russia.

PALEONTOLOGISTS AT WORK

Some hard-working scientists were on the team that found *Psittacosaurus.* These scientists were paleontologists (PAY-lee-un-TAWL-uh-jists). Paleontologists are people who study the fossil remains of ancient living things. They try to learn more about plants and animals that lived long ago. This can be an exciting—but often difficult—job.

Some paleontologists do lots of field work. This means they travel to areas where they expect to find fossils and work "out in the field." Sometimes they stay for weeks, or even months, living in those areas. They might have to endure long days in the hot sun or in the freezing cold. They might have to put up with heavy rains, mosquitoes, wild animals, and broken equipment. But if they discover a new dinosaur, all these troubles seem worthwhile.

Some paleontologists work in laboratories. They might look at dinosaur fossils under a microscope. By doing this, they can sometimes figure out how quickly a dinosaur grew, whether it was ever sick, and even how old it was when it died.

Some paleontologists

work as teachers. They show students how to hunt for fossils and how to tell all the different dinosaur bones apart. They also explain to the public how dinosaurs lived and died.

Paleontologists don't just work on dinosaurs, though. They study all kinds of ancient animals and plants. Some paleontologists study inverte-brates (in-VUR-tuh-bruts), or animals without back-bones. These scientists work on the fossils of ancient corals, clams, and spiders. Other paleontologists study plants. They hunt for fossilized leaves, flowers, and even seeds. Then they can tell us about ancient plant life. Being a paleontologist is exciting, but it also takes lots of hard work.

CHAPTER FOUR

BUILT TO EAT PLANTS

Scientists believe that *Psittacosaurus* was a plant eater, or herbivore (URB-uh-vore). They have many reasons to believe this. The dinosaur's head, teeth, hands, feet, and body shape all point to it leading a plant-eating life.

Plant eaters such as Psittacosaurus *made up about 65 percent of the dinosaur population.*

The dinosaur's head came to a pointed beak. The beak was perfect for tearing tough plants from the ground and for snapping twigs and branches from bushes. When the dinosaur ate, its leaf-shaped teeth acted like scissors and chopped up the plant material. If *Psittacosaurus* had been a meat eater, its mouth would have been packed from front to back with sharp, piercing teeth.

The hands and feet of *Psittacosaurus* also hint at a plant-eating life. The hands and feet of fierce meat-eating dinosaurs had long, sharp, curved claws. Such claws were perfect for holding down **prey** and tearing flesh. However, *Psittacosaurus* did not have such fierce claws. Its little claws were better for handling plants.

Psittacosaurus probably was not a slender dinosaur. Most dinosaurs that ate plants were thick-bodied. They had wide bodies because they had big, long **digestive** systems inside. Plant materials are very hard to break down. So plant-eating dinosaurs

needed a lot of room inside to handle the job.

Paleontologists have found *Psittacosaurus* skeletons that contain

rocks called gastroliths (GASS-troh-liths). Some plant-eating

dinosaurs swallowed gastroliths. The rocks stayed in the dinosaurs'

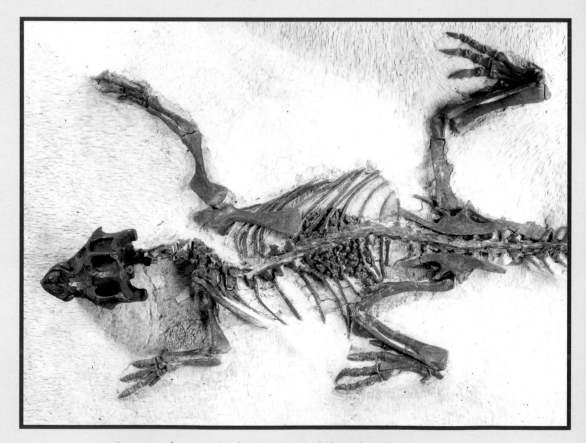

Scientists discovered a fossilized gastrolith within this Psittacosaurus *rib cage. Eating rocks might not sound yummy to you, but the process played an important role in the digestion of plant-eating dinosaurs.*

Chemicals in the dinosaur's stomach helped to wear down gastroliths and caused them to become smooth and shiny.

stomachs. As the dinosaurs moved about, the rocks pounded food into mush. Over time, the rocks themselves wore down and became small and useless. Then the dinosaur had to swallow more rocks. Gastroliths helped plant-eating dinosaurs to break down their food. Meat-eating dinosaurs did not have them.

IS THERE DINOSAUR FOOD IN YOUR NEIGHBORHOOD?

Psittacosaurus was just one of the many plant-eating dinosaurs. Many of the plants that dinosaurs ate no longer exist today. However, some are still around. In fact, some of the dinosaurs' favorite foods might be growing in your neighborhood!

Plant-eating dinosaurs often munched on mosses and ferns (below). Dinosaurs that were built low to the ground especially liked these short, soft plants. Such plants are common today and are usually found in shady or damp places.

Cycads (SY-kadz) are plants that look like short palm trees. *Psittacosaurus* surely would have needed gastroliths to break down these hardy plants. Their leaves are long, sharp, and very tough. Today, many cycads grow in warm areas.

Ginkgo (GING-koe) trees were another dinosaur favorite. These trees have soft, fan-shaped leaves (above). Today, people often grow them in their yards and gardens. Dinosaurs also ate from cone-bearing trees much like our modern-day pines. These trees are found almost everywhere and are able to grow in poor and rocky soil.

The next time you walk down the street, look around. You'll probably see dinosaur food everywhere!

CHAPTER FIVE

PSITTACOSAURUS AND ITS RELATIVES

Psittacosaurus was a member of a large group of dinosaurs called the ceratopsians (SEHR-uh-TOP-see-unz). The ceratopsians lived in Asia and North America. Their heads were heavily armored. Some had horns sticking out from their faces. Some had a large, bony collar, or frill, spreading out around the neck.

All of the ceratopsians were plant eaters. Each had a hard beak with a downward-curving tip. They ate some of the toughest plant material around. Many people are familiar with one

Styracosaurus (sty-RAK-oh-SAWR-uhss) was a ceratopsian that lived in North America about 70 million years ago.

Unlike Psittacosaurus, Triceratops *was a large ceratopsian that weighed up to 6 tons. When threatened,* Triceratops *used its horns to charge its enemy.*

ceratopsian, called *Triceratops* (try-SEHR-uh-tops). *Leptoceratops* (LEP-toe-SEHR-uh-tops) and little *Bagaceratops* (BAG-uh-SEHR-uh-tops) were other ceratopsians.

Scientists believe that the ceratopsians were related to each other. Many of them looked alike. But how can *Psittacosaurus* be a ceratopsian? It looked nothing like the big, three-horned *Triceratops*.

Some scientists believe *Psittacosaurus* was one of the very first

ceratopsians. Others believe that *Psittacosaurus* was a more distant

relative of the group. It had a triangular head and a pointed beak.

It had short horns poking out from its face. It also had a small bony

ridge across the back of its head—a sort of tiny frill. Scientists

believe that over millions of years, some of these features became

larger. So as time went on, ceratopsians with remarkable frills began

to **evolve.** Some had enormous horns on their faces. There were

also huge ceratopsians that had beaked heads weighing several hun-

dred pounds.

Ceratopsians walked the earth for about 55 million years. Several

different kinds evolved and then died out. Finally, 65 million years

ago, they—and all of the other dinosaurs—disappeared forever.

CHAPTER SIX

THE WORLD OF
PSITTACOSAURUS

When *Psittacosaurus* was alive, the world was completely

different from the one we know today. The dinosaur

lived in a time called the Cretaceous (kree-TAY-shuss) period.

During that period, the **continents** were much closer together

During the Cretaceous period, the earth's continents were packed much closer together. It's even possible that some dinosaurs simply walked from one continent to another.

Deinonychus *(DY-no-NY-kuhss) was a deadly killer not only because of its claws and teeth, but also because it was highly intelligent.*

than they are today. North America was closer to Europe. South

America was closer to Africa. Because of this crowding, the Atlantic

Ocean was much smaller.

Reptiles were plentiful during the Cretaceous period, and dinosaurs were common. While *Psittacosaurus* lived in Asia, other dinosaurs roamed elsewhere. In North America, *Deinonychus* trotted about. It ran on two legs, holding its terrible "killing claw" toes up from the ground as it ran. In Africa, the sail-backed *Ouranosaurus* (oo-RAN-uh-SAWR-uhss) quietly searched for plants. In Australia, the heavily plated *Minmi* (MIN-mee) plodded along.

During the Cretaceous period, dinosaurs were everywhere. It was truly the "Age of Reptiles." But things are different now. Today, we live in the "Age of Mammals." Mammals such as rabbits and squirrels play in our yards. Mammals such as dogs, cats, and hamsters live in our homes. Mammals such as zebras, giraffes, tigers, and elephants live in Africa and Asia. The days of the ruling reptiles are gone forever.

Glossary

ancient (AYN-shunt) Something that is ancient is very old. Paleontologists study ancient life.

continents (KON-tuh-nuhntz) Continents are the earth's seven large land-masses. *Psittacosaurus* lived on the continent of Asia.

digestive (dye-JESS-tiv) Digestive refers to eating and processing food. *Psittacosaurus* had a large digestive system.

evolve (i-VOLV) To evolve means to change at a slow pace, often over a long period of time. During the Cretaceous period, ceratopsians with remarkable frills began to evolve.

fossils (FOSS-uhlz) Fossils are things that are left behind by ancient plants or animals. In the early 1900s, paleontologists found *Psittacosaurus* fossils in Mongolia.

preserve (pri-ZURV) To preserve something means to save it. Paleontologists thought that the Mongolian desert might preserve fossils well.

prey (PRAY) Prey are animals that are hunted and eaten by other animals. *Psittacosaurus* did not have sharp claws for holding down prey.

reptile (REP-tile) A reptile is an animal that breathes air, has a backbone, and usually is covered with scales or plates. Reptiles were abundant during the Cretaceous period.

Did You Know?

▸ Some scientists believe that *Psittacosaurus* fought off its enemies by swinging its head into them.

▸ The full name of the first *Psittacosaurus* ever found is *Psittacosaurus mongoliensis* (mon-GO-lee-EN-sis), meaning "parrot lizard from Mongolia."

▸ *Psittacosaurus* may have lived and traveled in herds for safety and protection. Scientists believe other kinds of ceratopsians also lived this way.

▸ The Greek word *psittakos,* meaning "parrot," appears not only in *Psittacosaurus,* but also in other scientific terms. For instance, parrots and parakeets belong to a group of birds called the psittaciforms (SIT-uh-kuh-forms), and a disease called parrot fever is also called psittacosis (SIT-uh-KO-siss).

How to Learn More

AT THE LIBRARY

Barrett, Paul. *National Geographic Dinosaurs.* Washington, D.C.: National Geographic Society, 2001.

Lambert, David, Darren Naish, and Liz Wyse. *Dinosaur Encyclopedia.* New York: DK Publishing, 2001.

Palmer, Douglas, and Barry Cox (editors). *The Simon & Schuster Encyclopedia of Dinosaurs & Prehistoric Creatures: A Visual Who's Who of Prehistoric Life.* New York: Simon & Schuster, 1999.

ON THE WEB

Visit our home page for lots of links about *Psittacosaurus*:

http://www.childsworld.com/links.html

NOTE TO PARENTS, TEACHERS, AND LIBRARIANS: We routinely verify our Web links to make sure they're safe, active sites—so encourage your readers to check them out!

PLACES TO VISIT OR CONTACT

AMERICAN MUSEUM OF NATURAL HISTORY
*To view numerous dinosaur fossils, as well
as the fossils of several ancient mammals*
Central Park West at 79th Street
New York, NY 10024-5192
212/769-5100

CARNEGIE MUSEUM OF NATURAL HISTORY
*To view a variety of dinosaur skeletons, as well
as fossils related to other extinct animals*
4400 Forbes Avenue
Pittsburgh, PA 15213
412/622-3131

DINOSAUR NATIONAL MONUMENT
*To view a huge deposit of dinosaur bones
in a natural setting*
Dinosaur, CO 81610-9724
or
DINOSAUR NATIONAL MONUMENT (QUARRY)
11625 East 1500 South
Jensen, UT 84035
435/781-7700

MUSEUM OF THE ROCKIES
To see real dinosaur fossils, as well as robotic replicas
Montana State University
600 West Kagy Boulevard
Bozeman, MT 59717-2730
406/994-2251 or 406/994-DINO (3466)

NATIONAL MUSEUM OF NATURAL HISTORY
(SMITHSONIAN INSTITUTION)
*To see several dinosaur exhibits and special
behind-the-scenes tours*
10th Street and Constitution Avenue NW
Washington, DC 20560-0166
202/357-2700

The Geologic Time Scale

CAMBRIAN PERIOD

Date: 540 million to 505 million years ago
Most major animal groups appeared by the end of this period. Trilobites were common and algae became more diversified.

ORDOVICIAN PERIOD

Date: 505 million to 440 million years ago
Marine life became more diversified. Crinoids and blastoids appeared, as did corals and primitive fish. The first land plants appeared. The climate changed greatly during this period—it began as warm and moist, but temperatures ultimately dropped. Huge glaciers formed, causing sea levels to fall.

SILURIAN PERIOD

Date: 440 million to 410 million years ago
Glaciers melted, sea levels rose, and the earth's climate became more stable. Fish with jaws first appeared, as did the first freshwater fish. Plants with vascular systems developed. This means they had parts that helped them to conduct food and water.

DEVONIAN PERIOD

Date: 410 million to 360 million years ago
Fish became more diverse, as did land plants. The first trees and forests appeared at this time, and the earliest seed-bearing plants began to grow. The first land-living vertebrates and insects appeared. Fossils also reveal evidence of the first ammonites and amphibians. The climate was warm and mild.

CARBONIFEROUS PERIOD

Date: 360 million to 286 million years ago
The climate was warm and humid, but cooled toward the end of the period. Coal swamps dotted the landscape, as did a multitude of ferns. The earliest reptiles walked the earth. Pelycosaurs such as *Edaphosaurus* evolved toward the end of the Carboniferous period.

PERMIAN PERIOD

Date: 286 million to 248 million years ago
Algae, sponges and corals were common on the ocean floor. Amphibians and reptiles were also prevalent at this time, as were seed-bearing plants and conifers. However, this period ended with the largest mass extinction on earth. This may have been caused by volcanic activity or the formation of glaciers and the lowering of sea levels.

TRIASSIC PERIOD

Date: 248 million to 208 million years ago
The climate during this period was warm and dry. The first true mammals appeared, as did frogs, salamanders, and lizards. Evergreen trees made up much of the plant life. The first dinosaurs, including *Coelophysis*, walked the earth. In the skies, pterosaurs became the earliest winged reptiles to take flight. In the seas, ichthyosaurs and plesiosaurs made their appearance.

JURASSIC PERIOD

Date: 208 million to 144 million years ago
The climate of the Jurassic period was warm and moist. The first birds appeared at this time, and plant life was more diverse and widespread. Although dinosaurs didn't even exist in the beginning of the Triassic period, they ruled the earth by Jurassic times. *Allosaurus, Apatosaurus, Archaeopteryx, Brachiosaurus, Compsognathus, Diplodocus, Ichthyosaurus, Plesiosaurus,* and *Stegosaurus* were just a few of the prehistoric creatures that lived during this period.

CRETACEOUS PERIOD

Date: 144 million to 65 million years ago
The climate of the Cretaceous period was fairly mild. Many modern plants developed, including those with flowers. With flowering plants came a greater diversity of insect life. Birds further developed into two types: flying and flightless. Prehistoric creatures such as *Ankylosaurus, Edmontosaurus, Iguanodon, Maiasaura, Oviraptor, Psittacosaurus, Spinosaurus, Triceratops, Troodon, Tyrannosaurus rex,* and *Velociraptor* all existed during this period. At the end of the Cretaceous period came a great mass extinction that wiped out the dinosaurs, along with many other groups of animals.

TERTIARY PERIOD

Date: 65 million to 1.8 million years ago
Mammals were extremely diversified at this time, and modern-day creatures such as horses, dogs, cats, bears, and whales developed.

QUATERNARY PERIOD

Date: 1.8 million years ago to today
Temperatures continued to drop during this period. Several periods of glacial development led to what is known today as the Ice Age. Prehistoric creatures such as glyptodonts, mammoths, mastodons, *Megatherium,* and sabre-toothed cats roamed the earth. A mass extinction of these animals occurred approximately 10,000 years ago. The first human beings evolved during the Quaternary period.

Index

Age of Mammals, 27
Age of Reptiles, 27

Bagaceratops, 23
beak, *6*, 10, 17, 24
body, 16, 17–18

ceratopsians, 22–24, *22*
claws, 17
continents, 25–26
Cretaceous period, 25–27, *25*
cycads, 21

Deinonychus, *26*, 27
digestive system, 17–19

eggs, 13
eyes, 10

feet, 16, 17
ferns, 20, *20*
fingers, 9, *9*
food, 16, *16*, 17, 19, 20–21
fossils, 11, 14, 15, *15*, 18

gastroliths, 18–19, *18*, *19*, 21
gingko trees, 21, *21*

hands, 9, 16, 17
head, 7, *7*, 9–10, *10*, 13, 16, 17, 24
herbivores, 16

horns, 10, 24

invertebrates, 15

jaw, 9

legs, 8, 9
Leptoceratops, 23

Minmi, 27
Mongolia, 11–13, *12*
mosses, 20

name, 7
nostrils, 10

Osborn, Henry Fairfield, 11, 13, *13*
Ouranosaurus, 27

paleontologists, 14–15, *15*, 18
Psittacosaurus, 4, *6*, *7*, *8*, *9*, *10*, *16*, 18

size, *4*, 8, *8*
Styracosaurus, *22*

tail, 8
teeth, 10, 16, 17
Triceratops, 23, *23*

weight, 8
Wong (Mongolian driver), 13

About the Author

Susan H. Gray has bachelor's and master's degrees in zoology and has taught college-level courses in biology. She first fell in love with fossil hunting while studying paleontology in college. In her 25 years as an author, she has written many articles for scientists and researchers, and many science books for children. Susan enjoys gardening, traveling, and playing the piano. She and her husband, Michael, live in Cabot, Arkansas.